MW00939575

For Shawn and Dede
God has a plan for you!
Jeremiah 29:11

Linda S. Carter

THE SMALL FINE PRINT

God's Plan for Your Vision

Linda S. Carter

WESTBOW
PRESS®
A DIVISION OF THOMAS NELSON
& ZONDERVAN

WestBow Press books may be ordered through booksellers or by contacting:

WestBow Press
A Division of Thomas Nelson & Zondervan
1663 Liberty Drive
Bloomington, IN 47403
www.westbowpress.com
844-714-3454

Interior Image Credit: Mia Little/Little Designs Creative Studio
Little Designs Creative Studiio

ISBN: 978-1-6642-1695-2 (sc)
ISBN: 978-1-6642-1694-5 (hc)
ISBN: 978-1-6642-1696-9 (e)

Library of Congress Control Number: 2020925401

Print information available on the last page.

WestBow Press rev. date: 03/04/2021

For Tamara Renée

THE SMALL
FINE PRINT

CONTENTS

INTRODUCTION
Trust and Believe

———

"You better be good to her before she dies." This is how my 10-year-old self remembers that repetitive voice from within that spoke every time I was angry and swearing never to speak to my older sister again. At the time, I didn't understand why I was being given this warning, and it would be many years later before I understood what it meant. You see, my 12-year-old sister had been diagnosed with a brain tumor at the age of 5, and after a number of brain surgeries, the last left her comatose and unable to awaken. As sisters, our lives, which were so intricately woven together, would be forever changed. We would never celebrate the achievement of her high school graduation. We would never sit and talk about a bad break-up with her boyfriend. We would never plan her wedding day. We would never celebrate the birth of her first child. None of these things happened because my sister died shortly after that last surgery in October 1971.

This life that I had not yet had the opportunity to claim as my own had been changed in ways that I, as a child, could not understand. There would be many years of trials and hardships before I would look back on my sister's death as a defining moment of my life. Let me be clear, I know that I am not the only person who has had a childhood encounter of hearing God, and my story is not so incredible or different. What is incredible is the common thread of a vocal God in the everyday experiences of human existence. Before you ask me what I mean by this, please let me state it more clearly: God has a *purposeful plan* He reveals, in part, through divinely appointed moments. These divine moments are unique to God who speaks to each of us in visions, dreams, prayer, and worship. We must trust and believe that it is God and that He is unfolding His plan. More importantly, we must learn how to listen to God, so we know what to expect, and what is expected in our pursuit of His plans for our future.

————

There were many others before you or me who struggled with the idea of God's plan. The struggle is commonly rooted in not knowing exactly what the plan is and how to navigate it on our terms. This is what the prophet Jeremiah struggled with while he and the people of God were in captivity. He went to God for answers that would address the chaos created by false prophets. When he asked God what he was expected to do in what seemed like an impossible situation, Jeremiah recalls that God answered Him as the Creator of all things including the plan.

> "For I know the plans I have for you," declares the Lord, "plans to prosper you and not to harm you, plans to give you hope and a future." (Jeremiah 29:11 NIV)

Jeremiah's revelation in this divine moment was in hearing God had a plan. Although the details were not disclosed, he believed God's plan would provide redemption, restoration and reconciliation for the people. Jeremiah, in the midst of crisis not only heard God but trusted a plan that had been conceived long before their captivity. This plan, constructed by the Master Architect, contained solutions for their current situation and sustainable resources for their future and prosperity. Here is the takeaway: Jeremiah's encounter with God, as well as my own personal encounters, revealed that God has designed a plan for the future. Even though this life will have its unexpected and uninvited challenges, our hope lies in knowing there is a purposeful plan, and we have to trust and believe in it.

————

The death of my sister was difficult for me as a child. It left me with an emptiness that I was not spiritually, mentally or emotionally mature enough to make sense of at the time. Nevertheless, God had a plan for me that would cultivate a vision for my future. The trauma of losing a sibling did not thwart my life's successes nor did it destroy me or leave me in a perpetual state of hopelessness. In hindsight, I understand these experiences were guiding me toward God, who cultivated both my relationship with Him and my vision. Then, it was not always apparent that God had a *spiritual blueprint* for me, but He did, and it was indelibly inked in *the small fine print* as both His plan and His promise for my life.

1

CHASING THE VOICE

Did God Really Say That?

And the Lord God commanded the man,
saying, "Of every tree of the garden you may
freely eat; but of the tree of the knowledge
of good and evil you shall not eat, for in the
day that you eat of it you shall surely die."
(Genesis 2:16-17)

Throughout my life and especially in my twenties, I was
always trying to make sense of the *something told me* or *a
strange feeling* that I had about situations I was facing. These
two responses were usually in regard to some circumstance
or a reaction to a decision I needed to make in the immediate
future. What is evident now is that I lacked the insight to

realize that this was God. In today's context, if someone says to me anything that sounds remotely similar to these two statements, I will respond by naming that *something told me* or *a strange feeling* as God's voice and the Holy Spirit's nudging. In my everyday encounters and conversations with family, friends and colleagues, I am often reminded that this way of reasoning has become a part of our norm. Are we perplexed and unsure about the presence of holiness? Could God actually be concerned enough about us to give both wisdom and warning? Well, before I answer with an affirmative *yes*, I would like us to consider Eve, who was the first woman, the first wife, and the first mother of all of humanity.

As the first woman, Eve was in a unique situation. She was not exposed to the influences of the world in the way we are as children. There were no human parents, grandparents, or siblings to convince her of or commit her to an ideology other than what God had purposed, planned, and envisioned for her life. Therefore, whenever Eve heard a voice, there was absolutely no question that it was God's voice. God's voice was familiar to her. It was neither *something* nor *strange*. The wisdom and warning given to her by God's own voice was clear and concise. Eve and Adam were never to eat from the tree of the knowledge of good and evil. The plan for all human life was embodied in this one unique tree. This forbidden fruit was prohibited by God. However, Eve used the profound power of her choice to deliberately disobey God and His perfect plan for humanity. By doing so, she ignored the wisdom and warning given to her, and to Adam, and changed the course of human history from one of immortality to one of mortality. Even now, there are many biblical scholars who may argue that because Eve did not receive God's instruction firsthand, she did not understand the magnitude of the consequences of her decision. I have often heard this argument in many church, ministry, and Christian circles. My position on this argument is: If God said it to Adam, who personified the entirety of humanity, then the wisdom and warning applied to all of humanity, including Eve. To emphasize my position, Jesus Christ did not endure the cross for some but for all.

There is no way to know what Eve was thinking when she exercised such great power and ate the forbidden fruit. There is no way to understand her motives or desires because they are not recorded in any account of scripture.

Yet the question that remains for me is whose voice was Eve chasing? Before I attempt to give any reasoning to this question, let's look at the dramatic manner in which she recalls God's instruction:

> Now the serpent was more cunning than any beast of the field which the Lord God had made. And he said to the woman, "Has God indeed said, 'You shall not eat of every tree of the garden'?" And the woman said to the serpent, "We may eat the fruit of the trees of the garden; "but of the fruit of the tree which is in the midst of the garden, God has said, 'You shall not eat it, nor shall you touch it, lest you die.'" Then the serpent said to the woman, "You will not surely die. "For God knows that in the day you eat of it your eyes will be opened, and you will be like God, knowing good and evil." (Genesis 3:1-5)

In the scripture quoted in the introduction of this chapter, there is no mention of touching the tree of the knowledge of good and evil. Nonetheless, Eve recalls this detail. There are several rhetorical questions I would like to present as a part of this discussion. Is it possible there had been some discussion between Eve and Adam about this specific tree? Is it possible Eve was tempted *before* the encounter with the serpent? Is it possible Eve was chasing God's voice in her own intimate and divinely appointed moment? In other words, is it possible Eve wanted God to intervene and keep her from disobedience? Again, none of these questions can be answered unequivocally because there are no historical references given in Eve's biblical account that would validate any of these scenarios. What we do know is that Eve's decision in the Garden of Eden changed the course of human history, and heartache and hardship befell us. Eve's willful disobedience moved all of humanity from spiritual clarity to spiritual obscurity, and we began to hear and attribute God's voice to *a strange feeling* or that *something* that speaks from within us at the point of decision. However, what did not change was, is, and will forever be God who has forged a plan for each of us.

Now that I am far removed from the twenty-something years and I have no real excuse for missing the wisdom and warnings of God, I will admit there are still times when I do. The reason for this is that I have the tendency to make plans, and sometimes I do so without consulting God. This is because I see myself as the ultimate planner. I plan for my husband. I plan for my family. I plan for my friends. I plan for church and other organizations. I plan for everything in my life because I know I am good at it, and can get things done effectively and efficiently, right? At least this is the logic I use to drive my motives for planning. To be completely transparent, I don't do well with going with the flow. And spontaneity drives me to become unglued. This is because for me not having a plan means not having complete control, and control provides me with a sense of safety. Although in reality, being in control of your life is not how faith actually works. There have been times when I have thought, *this is the perfect plan.* Of course, God probably laughs at the absurdness of it all. This is why we should exercise caution when we reason from a place of knowing. When you know you are good at something, it can be difficult to hear God. Your choices are driven only by your own knowledge, and it can become hard for you to be guided by God in a direction that He has intended for you. It can also cause you to question whether it is God's voice you are hearing at all. It is the same dilemma Eve faced when she encountered temptation in the Garden of Eden.

I would love to tell you that now that I am a mature Christian, I can hear God as clearly as Adam and Eve did the day that sin entered into the human experience, but it would not be true. In my quiet moments with God, whether through personal bible study, prayer, or worship, I speak to God and have learned to listen for God to speak to me. I am deliberate in seeking His direction, guidance, and instruction in His own voice. I am chasing God for His plans for my vision. Plans that God has spoken clearly and concisely to me, and that I hear without question and receive without reservation. Plans that God has written for me before I was born or known to my parents. Plans that are indelibly inked by God in *the small fine print*.

———

What is *the small fine print*? *The small fine print* is a multi-dimensional spiritual blueprint of God's plan for your vision. It is constructed by God and is designed specifically for you. The spiritual blueprint materializes as a visual guide of action steps to achieve your vision as the desired result, and is made viable, as a result of your immutable faith. As a viable plan, it enables you to see your vision with high visibility, and figuratively tears away anything that obstructs your vision and God's plan from your view.

In the context of this and the following chapters, God's plan is not to be understood as an exhaustive examination or conclusion of the providential nature of God. It is rather a reference to the divine relationship between God and humanity, and the blessings that the relationship invites. Therefore, *the small fine print* helps you visualize the process for achieving your vision as the desired result, and as a manifested blessing of God's plan.

2

LET'S TALK MAPPING
Hear The Plan, See The Vision

———

Where there is no vision, the people perish: but he that keepeth the law, happy is he. (Proverbs 29:18 KJV)

As a college student, I planned to become the next Oprah. I planned to finish my bachelor's degree and land a job as a local television news anchor. I planned to anchor for a couple of years until I was discovered by a national media organization. I planned for the national media exposure to be the means to Oprah status, and I planned for the rest to be history. This sounds pretty unrealistic, right? Well at that time, I was still in my twenties and this was my actual plan. I had my news video, portfolio, and references all set to go, but what I did not have was foresight or a vision. Needless to say, I was never hired as a local television news anchor and never received a call from a national media organization. This was because I failed to understand that every plan should have a vision as the core goal, and a process for realizing it. This process for realizing a vision is what I have named as *mapping*. I will talk more about the process of mapping later in this chapter, but for now, let's turn our attention to the importance of having a *vision*.

The purpose of having a vision is to help you visualize a plan for your future goals. When you can visualize your plan, you see the course of action needed to achieve the result. Visualizing your plan also means aligning your vision to God's plan, and this is crucial to your success. When you align your vision, you gain spiritual insight and recognize ministry gifts that equip, and empower you, and help you to discern existing resources needed to realize your vision. A good example of the value in aligning your vision with God's plan is shared in the story of Esther.

Esther's vision of her life was to live quietly and comfortably. She had already achieved both safety and satisfaction as the new Queen of Persia, but God had a plan and a purpose for her that she had not considered. Let's take a closer look at Esther's story.

> When Esther's words were reported to Mordecai, he sent back this answer: "Do not think that because you are in the king's house you alone of all the Jews will escape. For if you remain silent at this time, relief and deliverance for the Jews will arise from another place, but you and your father's family will perish. And who knows but that you have come to royal position for such a time as this?" Then Esther sent this reply to Mordecai: "Go, gather together all the Jews who are in Susa, and fast for me. Do not eat or drink for three days, night or day. I and my maids will fast as you do. When this is done, I will go to the king, even though it is against the law. And if I perish, I perish." (Esther 4:12-16 NIV)

Esther's story concludes with her being victorious. She is credited with saving her people from complete annihilation.

Her task was both dangerous and difficult. Nevertheless, Esther faced her fears, challenged the laws of the land, and proceeded with courageous faith. The part of her story that is often overlooked is the process she used to align her vision with God's plan. Esther needed to hear the plan to see the vision.

Before Esther's victory was secured, her relative Mordecai who was responsible for her rise to royalty, had urged her to act on behalf of her people. In her back-and-forth conversations with Mordecai, Esther realized she was facing a serious dilemma. She needed a plan that would ultimately save her people. Saving her people was the desired result. What Esther did next was crucial to her victory and her future. Esther began aligning her vision by fasting for wisdom, revelation, and knowledge. She realized that her crisis was well beyond human ability or natural intervention. Fasting was a familiar spiritual discipline that was often used for spiritual insight and breakthrough. When Esther emerged from her fast, she had the spiritual insight needed to implement a strategic vision plan that was fully aligned with God's plan. Spiritual insight is key to uncovering resources that God is making available to achieve your vision and the desired result.

Esther's story is unique because she is a young and inexperienced heroine. Her act of courageous faith is a testament to her reliance on her relationship with God, even though God is not mentioned once in her biblical account. Did God intervene in response to their relationship? Was her corporate fast always a part of God's providential plan? Although there is no concise biblical evidence to support one of these positions above the other, I believe both perspectives are applicable. Neither perspective would have any valuable insight if Esther had not chosen to act. What is clear is that Esther's fast gave her an ability to hear and see a strategic vision plan to save her people. The key takeaway from Esther's story is your faith, familiar spiritual disciplines like fasting and prayer, and your reliance on your relationship with God, are significant to the process of aligning your vision with God's plan. This is important to keep in mind as you learn the process of mapping and aligning your vision.

Now, let's dive into the process of mapping a vision. I want to share with you how I began the process of mapping my vision with God's plan. Before we had access to a Global Positioning System (GPS), the way a person traveled across the city, region, state, or country was with a road map. The road map was usually this very large multi-folded, two-dimensional paper compass of roads, rural routes, and interstate highways. What I most remember about reading a road map is that it required a level of skill to interpret the geography the map represented. But if you didn't know how to read a map, it was just a colorful oversized piece of paper with numbers, road names, zig-zagging lines, and a compass key in the bottom corner. Remember my Oprah plan at the beginning of this chapter? That Oprah plan was a road map that I could neither read nor interpret at the time. It wasn't because the Oprah plan was impossible, but because I was unable to make sense of a plan devised without spiritual insight or resources. In fact, I had no resources or support to begin the task of devising a vision plan, and not because I was twenty-something, but because there were other things on my plate. Here is the short list:

- Single parent.
- Limited support systems.

- No financial resources.
- Survivor of domestic violence.
- No genuine relationship with God.

This was the list of my reality and not the list of my plan. Like the description of the map above it was just zig-zagging lines. This was because God, who I so desperately needed, had not yet turned those zig-zagging lines into visible roads. In my mind, visible roads would guide me to a destination to become the new and improved Oprah. In hindsight, what I wanted and how I envisioned achieving it were two different things. There was no hocus pocus to it. There was only the hard work of learning how to turn a vision into a working strategy that could be mapped and aligned with God's plan, and the intricate details of *the small fine print.*

The task of mapping is a process. It will help you visualize your core goal, a workable strategy, and guide the progressive alignment of your vision with God's plan. The mapping process has four primary tasks:

1. To help you clarify the specific goals of your vision.
2. To help you identify your starting point.

3. To help you confirm the resources needed to achieve the desired result.

4. To help you develop the sequence of steps into workable strategies to successfully complete your vision goals.

When you begin the process of mapping your vision, you are demonstrating your readiness for the plans God has established for you. This also means you have completed the four primary tasks above. As a result, you will have definitive goals, a starting point, the necessary resources, the sequence of steps, and spiritual insight regarding all tasks based on divine guidance. It also means your vision is fully aligned with God's plan.

How will you know your vision is aligned is with God's plan? You will know because God will confirm it with resources that are accessible and available. In other words, you must wait for God to confirm that right now is both the opportune time and optimal circumstances. Let me add one caution: if God has not confirmed resources, then wait! I firmly believe God has equipped us for every task or assignment He has confirmed. It is imperative that you are deliberate and intentional in avoiding the temptation to take action and proceed without God's confirmation.

———

The talent that my college professors recognized so many years ago for the national media stage were indeed gifts from God. However, the intended plan and purpose for my gifts were different than the Oprah plan I had conceived without any spiritual insight. Needless to say, I never achieved the Oprah plan to broadcast the news into the home of millions each day. Instead, I used my voice to comfort the sick, assure the grieved, and affirm the faithful. Those familiar with my voice would only know me as their Chaplain and Minister. Ministry was the vision that I would later draw into workable strategies to achieve the desired result. But before I could see the vision, I had to reconcile that I would not become the iconic voice of media broadcasts. Rather than claiming Oprah's success as the result I desired, I had to lean in and seek God for a vision that He had uniquely designed for me. This is why it is important to sit before God in prayerful contemplation. Once you have received spiritual confirmation, you will be ready to begin the process of drafting a *strategic vision map.*

———

The Bible verse referenced at the beginning of this chapter has often been interpreted as advocating for visionary leadership within the church. However, the meaning and scope of this verse is far more extensive. The writer concludes that without prophetic preaching, teaching, and obedience, the people will fall away from their relationship with God. This is because they will have no divine guidance for *how* to follow, *what to* do, and *when* to evade potential pitfalls. Remember Esther's fast? Her fast gave her an ability to hear and see a strategic vision plan to save her people. Her reliance on her relationship with God was significant to devising a strategy to save her people and align with God's foolproof plan. This is why positioning yourself through faithful obedience to *hear* the instruction and *see* the revelation of God's Word is crucial.

God's Word provides divinely appointed instructions that are foundational to your strategic vision planning. Without divine instruction, there can be no clarity of God's plan for your vision. There can also be no spiritual blueprint to guide you through the strategies to achieve your vision and the desired result. Therefore, revelation and divine instruction are especially relevant in the planning of your vision, the mapping process, and to visualizing a workable strategy needed to align with God's plan.

3

DRAFTING THE MAP
Creating A Visual

Then the Lord answered me and said: "Write the vision and make it plain on tablets, that he may run who reads it. For the vision is yet for an appointed time; but at the end it will speak, and it will not lie. Though it tarries, wait for it; because it will surely come, it will not tarry." (Habakkuk 2:2-3)

When I finished seminary, it became apparent to me rather quickly that my classmates had secured roles in churches and ministries across the country and around the world. By the time graduation day arrived, they had already accepted positions as pastors, worship leaders, youth ministers, and missionaries. It was as if they had drawn the map, charted the course, and arrived successfully at their destination. I, on the other hand, had discerned as a seminary student, that chaplaincy was my vision and ministry.

Chaplain ministry was once unfairly labeled as the *last resort* ministry. This was because clergy who were considered to be ill-equipped to lead a congregation were assigned to this ministry. As such, I would be starting my work in a ministry position that not one of my classmates desired. In fact, most of my classmates would proudly share that they were preparing for pastoral leadership in a church. They would wince at the thought of Chaplain ministry in a secular setting. And although this vision of ministry God had clarified for me would be challenging, I was more interested in succeeding with Him, than failing without Him.

———

Too often, when God gives an assignment, we start out zealously due to our own expectations and excitement. Zealousness can be blinding. It can cause a false sense of confidence and prevent us from getting all of the instructions needed to be successful. In such instances, we reach the divinely orchestrated destination without a plan of action for the assignment. To this point, consider this analogy: If I go to the store with a grocery list, then my list becomes a visual map of how to navigate the store, and a strategic plan of action to achieve the goal and the assignment. If I have eggs, milk, ice cream, and canned goods on my list, then the best course of action would be to locate the canned goods section first, and the frozen food section last. This course of action will decrease the possibility of unwanted outcomes like melting ice cream. However, without a list, my course of action is not strategic or well-planned. That means there is a greater chance of purchasing items I don't need and failing to select items I do need. The point of this analogy is to illustrate how a well-planned strategy is key to your success, and to the completion of specific tasks to achieve your desired result.

Another perspective of this analogy is to demonstrate how a well-planned strategy can be impacted by impulse and influence. Impulse and influence can thwart your success in achieving your vision. For example, the grocery list was a visual map used to navigate a planned approach to shopping. Although logic and reason were used as a part of the plan of action, it did not prohibit me from choosing items that were not on the list. If I were to detour from the list due to impulse or other factors, then my plan and strategy were unreliable. Thus, the grocery list was more of a draft than a completed plan with an impenetrable strategy. It is why I suggest you begin by drafting your strategic vision map first before you actually draw the map you will use as your guide. This will allow you to plan for unanticipated obstacles.

———

In the drafting stage, you will be able to sketch the path of your *vision strategy* as the navigational key to your strategic vision map. The vision strategy is developed by completing the four primary tasks to clarify information and provide you with valuable insight needed to develop strategies for a *plan of navigation*. The draft of the strategic vision map can then be used to troubleshoot potential roadblocks, wrong turns, and what seem like dead ends. Don't panic if your draft strategic vision map does not readily come together, because it is all part of the mapping process. Even asking

God for that immediate intervention to overcome obstacles is a part of the process. God's response may not be what you expect, but remember, He is the architect of the spiritual blueprint for this plan.

The draft of the strategic vision map evolves from the process of clarifying your vision, identifying a starting point, identifying resources, and evaluating spiritual support systems needed to achieve your vision. In the drafting stage, spiritual insight is used to develop a workable strategy to align your vision with God's plan. As you work through the process, you will be able to visualize the *small fine print* as a means for achieving your vision as the desired result.

The first step to the drafting process is to clarify your vision. You clarify your vision by defining the desired result of your core goal. This is achieved by narrowing the process to naming the specific desired result. When I did this, I clarified I was not going to become a media icon, social service worker, or pastor. These professional and ministry experiences were only meant to be foundational to my vision to become a Chaplain. What became clear to me was my primary ministry assignment would not be as a pastor to believers in a congregational setting.

Instead, my ministry would be to provide spiritual care as a pastoral Chaplain outside of the formal church structure. By clarifying my vision, I was able to draft a strategic vision map inclusive of theological training, clinical training, and spiritual formation, all of which provided a framework for the blueprint of my process. All of these experiences, training, and education were useful to clarifying my vision because they isolated my desired result.

The second step is to identify a starting point. Identifying the starting point is not as simple as it seems. This is because in order to define your starting point, you will need to visualize your path forward. My path was initially blocked by a full-time job, parenting two young children, and two adolescents, as well as managing a supportive role in my husband's successful career. In addition, I had assigned ministry responsibilities in my church. What I am getting at is this: when you are in the process of drafting and identifying your starting point for your strategic vision map, you will need to decide which access routes to your time to close, and which areas of your schedule to clear. Without making these two crucial decisions, it will be challenging to define your starting point and visualize a path forward.

With those decisions in mind, I had to determine how to address the need for work-life balance. Work-life balance establishes boundaries for your time. My need for firmer boundaries, enabled me to make adjustments. The adjustments were practical and accommodated my need for childcare, changes in the hours worked, and the re-assignment of ministry duties. The adjustments freed up my time, and time was what was needed to pursue my vision. The need for work-life balance also caused me to evaluate daily living habits that were negatively impacting my self-care needs. While I may have thought I was super woman, my physical, spiritual, and mental health were important, and needed to be included in all plans made to achieve my vision. Scheduling time for rest, exercise and prayer were essential in preserving my health and well-being. Therefore, I identified my starting point by clarifying priorities, establishing clear boundaries to appropriately realign my time, and creating a path forward by resolving any barriers to achieve my vision.

The third step is to identify resources that are available to achieve your vision. The task of identifying resources is both subjective and objective. Normally when you think about available resources to meet goals or achieve plans, you limit your thinking solely to finances and funding sources. Although financial resources are necessary, I want to encourage you to extend your focus further. You accomplish this by determining what areas of expertise or experiences you can deem as workable resources. Also assess the usefulness of the skills, talents, and gifts you bring to the process from your previous experiences, training, and comprehensive insight.

Other resources to consider are your relationships. Most relationships require an investment of your time. You will need to decide if people who share your time are a resource. Assess whether they contribute measurable support to advancing your strategies to achieve your vision. Once you have identified relational resources, you can incorporate them into your draft strategic vision map. What is important to remember is to not limit the scope of your resources. Oftentimes non-traditional resources are understated and are not as obvious to you. This is why identifying resources will require you to carefully consider your experiences, expertise, and relationships.

The fourth step is to evaluate your spiritual support

system. You will need to verify that your spiritual support system is structured to provide care before you categorize it as a resource. As a cautionary note, reciprocal sources of support may not be the best option. As it relates to my experience, faith was a consistent source of affirmation, guidance, and encouragement throughout the process. Unfortunately, my spiritual support system was not an optimal choice for my personal care needs, because it would have obligated me to spiritual care responsibilities. Due to this stipulation, I opted to use other sources for spiritual support as needed. This choice was consistent with the boundaries established to achieve my vision. Nonetheless, only you will know whether your faith or spiritual support system will be a valuable resource to achieving your vision.

Although these are not all of the areas to consider as possible resources, they should not be excluded. The following list serves as a quick reference guide to the process of identifying resources:

1. Begin by assessing the use of your time and the people, places, and things that require your attention. Establish boundaries as needed.

2. Assess the needs of those closest to you who will be most affected by your pursuit of your vision. Make adjustments as needed.

3. Meet with professional colleagues or your employer. Develop a schedule that is workable by freeing up time so you can pursue your vision.

4. Evaluate relationships with friends and other family. Determine their capacity to be resources for emotional, social, or physical support.

5. Determine how you will utilize spiritual support systems. As mentioned earlier, spiritual support systems should be beneficial and not reciprocal. Faith can also be utilized as a spiritual resource to guide, affirm, and encourage.

As you can see from my experience, the process of drafting a strategic vision map and completing the four primary tasks as a sequence of steps was important to creating a visual. As a result, I was able to clarify my vision and desired result, identify a starting point, determine resources, and evaluate and identify spiritual support. This is why it is paramount that you do not skip the process of working through the four primary tasks.

A drawing of my strategic vision map based on the above narrative follows. It is a rendering of my actual drawing and represents a part of my mapping process.

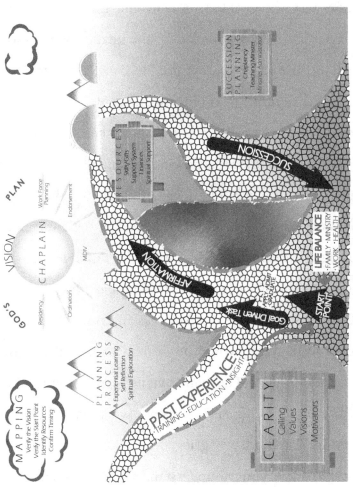

STRATEGIC VISION MAP

The scripture at the beginning of this chapter tells the story of the Prophet Habakkuk. He was distraught because of the sinfulness of God's chosen people. Habakkuk had pleaded with the people to repent, but they refused and ignored him. What Habakkuk did next is what most Christians in today's context do. He complained to God. But Habakkuk didn't just complain, he demanded that God discipline the people and put a stop to their wickedness. Habakkuk felt entitled to knowing the details of *when* God planned to take action. But once God gave him the vision, Habakkuk felt a sense of dread instead of the anticipated relief. There is familiar saying: *If you don't want to know the answer, then you probably shouldn't ask the question.*

God's response to Habakkuk was an assurance that the people's wickedness would be dealt with, but not in the way he had hoped. The Babylonians were to be used as God's chastening rod, and this is not what Habakkuk was expecting. God's answer grieved Habakkuk and left him frustrated and trying to understand God's plan. Here is a very important point: God always has a plan, but we may not be ready for the details. This is because God's timing is perfect, and by recognizing divine timing, you are indicating your readiness for the details. All of the spiritual encounters, gentle nudges, and quiet whispers you experienced are foundational and preparational moments for your vision. As such, you should feel assured that your vision has always been a part of God's plan, and He is making provisions for its success at the optimal time.

4

START HERE
The Vision Halo

If any of you lacks wisdom, he should ask
God, who gives generously to all without
finding fault, and it will be given to him.
(James 1:5 NIV)

There are always more details than you expect when you
start a new project or endeavor. This is especially true when
you begin the process of building a foundation for your
vision. When it comes to making your vision a functioning
reality, the details are everything. As this relates to the *vision
halo*, the details are specific correlating tasks that make
your vision halo function as the task center for your vision.
These correlating tasks also create the foundation for your

vision halo and *vision template*. The vision template precedes the vision halo and forms the outline for your vision. It is constructed with information gathered from experiential learning, self-reflection, and spiritual exploration. The story that follows serves as a personal example of how both my vision template and vision halo were developed.

One of my most teachable moments happened while I was a graduate student pursuing my Master of Divinity (MDiv) degree. At the time, I had not placed a lot of emphasis on creating the vision template for my vision halo. It wasn't until much later, that I realized how the experiential learning of the Clinical Pastoral Education (CPE) program had formulated an outline for my vision. A key requirement of the MDiv degree program was the completion of a unit of CPE. CPE was equivalent to one 4-credit-hour course. The purpose of CPE was to give seminary students practical life application experiences in ministry. Students had the option of completing their CPE in the hospital setting as a Chaplain or in the community in evangelism, pastoral leadership, or missionary-focused ministry. The CPE was an intensive ministry experience. I recognized later in self-reflection how foundational this experience was to my understanding of Chaplaincy as the desired result of my vision.

As a Chaplain student, I was given a week-long orientation and then charged with visiting patients and their families in the hospital setting. The broader goal of my charge was to provide comfort and support to patients without proselytizing. This meant I could not introduce God or Christian ideology nor convert, convict, or commit anyone to accepting my faith or my Christian beliefs. For me, this was a detail omitted from my brief orientation. I thought my primary role was to offer God as a source of hope and comfort to patients and their families. Surprisingly, every assumption I had about my role as a Chaplain was challenged. Then came that teachable moment. The Director of CPE explained to the students, who were just as dumbfounded as I, that it was an error in judgment to assume patients would be accepting of religious practices. Honestly, at that point, I was confused about the Chaplain assignment because none of my assumptions were correct. I actually had no clue as to how this was my vision or God's plan. What was clear is that Chaplain ministry required skills that I had not yet acquired or understood. My immediate response to this foregone conclusion, was to learn as much as possible about the vision I was actively pursuing. For this reason, the CPE experiential learning approach was paramount. If I was to capture the details needed to create a strategy for a functional version of my vision, and a foundation for my vision template, then I would need my call and my vision to be clear.

Let me take this opportunity to say a few more words about what it means to me to be called to a ministry assignment. The call is a summons to serve God and all people in meaningful ways. How a person defines the core reach of their call is through spiritual exploration with God, and by means of the Holy Spirit. As an example, the intention of a seminary education for me was to become a better Bible teacher. At this point, I had not engaged in the process of exploring my call to a specific ministry assignment. In my prayerful moments, personal study, and throughout seminary, God began to clarify His plan, but it was different than my original intention. What God clarified was the meaning of the *small fine print,* and it was a call to Chaplain ministry. Remember, the *small fine print* is a spiritual blueprint constructed by God and designed specifically for you. When you have clarity regarding your calling or purpose, then you will have the information needed to create your vision template.

To summarize, the purpose of the vision template is to form a foundational outline with details drawn from experiential learning, self-reflection, and spiritual exploration. These details are the action steps that make the vision halo function as the task center for your vision. Once the vision template is populated with information, you can begin creating the vision halo with your specific core goals.

The vision halo (see Illustration 1, Appendix) contains the specific tasks needed to achieve your vision. The vision halo has at its center your vision and core goals. Unique to the vision halo design is the position of the core goals as outliers to your vision. These core goals define the specific actions you will undertake to achieve the vision. In other words, they are co-dependent. Your vision is not viable until your core goals are in process or completed.

To create my vision halo, I needed to maximize the information gathered from the construction of the vision template. These narrowed goals were used to make the vision of becoming a Chaplain a *workable strategy.* A workable strategy is not a singular action, but a combination of corresponding actions to achieve core goals and ultimately your vision. Learning how to turn your vision into a workable strategy is an important step. To begin, focus on the completion of smaller tasks that correspond to core goals and make your vision viable. For example, completing the application process for seminary, assessing my financial resources, and adjusting my schedule to increase my availability, were smaller tasks of my core goal to achieve a MDiv. By tackling these smaller tasks, I was able to implement a workable strategy to begin completing a core goal within my vision halo. Therefore, the key to creating a workable strategy is to focus on smaller tasks considered crucial to the core goals of your vision.

As you look at the illustration of the vision halo, the smaller tasks have been identified as goal-driven tasks with an arrow at the base. The purpose of the task arrows will be discussed later in another chapter. However, once your core goals are activated by action on the smaller tasks, then your vision becomes viable. In summary, the vision halo contains your vision, and the core goals you will use to strategically plan and map your vision into a workable strategy to achieve your vision.

————

The scripture at the beginning of this chapter is a part of a pastoral letter written by James, the half-brother of Jesus. This letter to the Jews and Christians fleeing persecution, and scattered throughout the Roman Empire, was intended to encourage their faith and devotion to the teachings of Jesus. But James, in an unexpected bold and radical move, defines a believer's faith as a transformative power and divine connection to God. No other time in history had such access to God existed, but Jesus made this possible for His followers. James then offers this simple directive, *ask God*. With this directive, James ascribes to faith a means for divine connection and transformation to be possible.

Christians today are more likely to accept and believe their faith could produce supernatural results in a critical moment. Some theologians or biblical scholars might argue this approach to faith is too simplistic and does not give weighty consideration to God's sovereign nature. Nonetheless, whatever side of this debate you accept, James tells us to *ask as* empowered and embolden believers. Too often the problem is not that we expect too much help from God because of a robust faith, but rather that we expect too little due to a fragile faith. The point is faith not only produces divine connection with God, but also provides opportunities to *ask* God for the spiritual insight to transform your vision into a functioning reality.

5

IT'S IN THE CLOUD
The Mapping Cloud

"Therefore, I say to you, whatever things you ask when you pray, believe that you receive them, and you will have them." (Mark 11:24)

In this technology and information age in which we live, work, pray, and play is the existence of what we refer to as "the cloud." At a basic level of understanding, the cloud is a designated space on the internet where our personal information and data is stored. Essentially, the cloud is advanced technology. But because it is a part of the internet, we do not have complete control over it or sole ownership to it. The scope of the cloud and how it actually works is still foreign and even a little scary to me. What makes the cloud scary for me is not just my limited technology skills, but fear that some savvy hacker will take a peek at my personal life stored in the cloud and use it for some devious activities. While the cloud has its risks, it also has value. This is because what you store in the cloud is retained and rarely lost, even when information is temporarily inaccessible. Thus, in order to access the cloud, you must have some basic knowledge and understanding of how to operate a computer. You must also have some insight based on previous experience with uploading and downloading information and some common-sense application practices. All of these characteristics are important to gaining access to information stored in the cloud. Similarly, all of these characteristics are also important to accessing information stored in your *mapping cloud*.

The mapping cloud (see Illustration 2, Appendix) is a valuable part of your strategic vision map. The purpose of the mapping cloud is to cumulatively store your vision data and guiding strategies until they are complete and ready to be executed. Your vision data is a compilation of information based on your skills, training, and education, and forms your specific profile to plan your vision. Your guiding strategies are developed from information gathered by reviewing and revisiting your past experiences and influences to determine if, when, and how they can be mobilized to achieve your vision. Your vision data and guiding strategies are then organized into progressive steps as a part of your workable strategic vision plan.

Secondary to the mapping cloud is its use as a detailed checklist. The checklist functions to help you determine your readiness to proceed and keeps you on task. As such, you will need to verify your vision, resources, and starting point, and confirm the timing of your planned action steps. Therefore, the mapping cloud is multi-functional. It uses your vision data and guiding strategies as progressive steps to achieving your strategic vision plan.

The mapping cloud has four primary functions used to delineate progressive steps. The first function is to verify your vision. Verifying your vision is a process that challenges you to think critically as to *why* you believe your vision is the core goal and desired result. When you answer that question, it not only provides clarity relative to your calling, values, and motivation but also indicates your readiness for the next steps. However, you cannot verify until you are able to validate your vision as the intent of God's plan for you.

In my case, verifying the vision was a progressive process. When I enrolled in seminary, it was not in response to a calling to ministry but to improve my ability to serve. Service is what I most valued then, and service is what I continue to value now. More importantly, service was the *why* my vision to become a Chaplain made sense. At that particular time, I was actively serving in numerous capacities in the church. I had inadvertently reconciled my value for service with serving in the church setting. When given the opportunity to minister in a pastoral care capacity, I recognized ministry gifts and a spiritual equipping that I had not recognized before. It was not until my formal introduction to Chaplain ministry as a CPE student, that I was able to validate my vision as aligned with God's plan, and verify it as my core goal and desired result. Thus, verifying the vision was a result of my experiences, education and training. Remember, your vision data is based on your skills, training, and education, and guiding strategies are developed from review of past experiences and influences. By combining the vision data and guiding strategies, you will have the information needed to develop a workable strategy to achieve your vision. Further, having the answer to *why* is necessary for verifying your vision as your core goal and desired result.

The second function of the mapping cloud is to *verify* your starting point. You verify your starting point by applying knowledge drawn from past experiences and influences that will guide you to a definitive or justified decision. As you recall from Chapter 3, I discussed at length how to *identify* your starting point. As a conclusion, I shared that in order to identify your starting point you will need to clarify priorities, establish clear boundaries for your time, and resolve any barriers to achieving your vision. However, I did not expound on how past experiences and influences affect our decision-making. You verify your starting point by reviewing past experiences and influences which are key sources of knowledge. This experienced-based knowledge was useful to clarifying my abilities, amplifying my strengths, and magnifying my weaknesses. It influenced my thought process and reasoning in making decisions that were decisive and justified.

A personal example of justifying my decision occurred when I was in my final preparation for ordination. There were four other ministry peers in my group. All were male, and all had justified their decision to pastor congregations. Even though I never questioned their justified decisions, they on the other hand questioned mine. Here is where my experience-based knowledge served me well. Although they may have anticipated a response to their questioning, I offered them no debate, and provided no opportunities to validate or legitimate my justified decision. I had made a justified decision that was aligned with my call and God's plan. My experience-based knowledge developed as a journalist, social service worker, and administrator, as well as my insight as a woman in ministry, shaped and influenced my justified decision. Your identified starting point is verified by a justified decision and confirms your approach to achieving your vision.

The third function of the mapping cloud is to identify non-allocated resources you have available to realize your vision. As you will recall from Chapter 3, our discussion focused on resources such as your experiences, expertise, relationships, and spiritual support systems. As I pointed out, finances are an important and necessary resource to align your vision with God's plan. Identifying financial resources can be challenging because you can only consider funds not allocated to other obligations. As a caution, unless you have a financial overflow stored away, it would not be wise to attach additional stress to your allocated resources.

From a personal perspective, I was challenged to make a choice between my vision and my reality. I was making a good salary working full-time, and my salary was a secondary source of financial support for my family. My financial obligations included college tuition for our two oldest, private school tuition for our two youngest, and my seminary tuition. With a difficult decision before me, I needed to be realistic and consider all my options. It was clear that without additional revenue streams, I would need to delay taking action to advance my strategic vision map.

Dilemmas can be daunting, but faith, is a powerful and vital resource. Remember, my faith was a consistent source of affirmation, guidance and encouragement throughout the process. My response to this financial dilemma was to pray for resources, and then wait for God's instruction to either pursue or delay taking action. My prayers were not just for a resolve but were inclusive of petitions to reveal or provide opportunities for me to work for additional finances if needed. Through prayerful contemplation, God confirmed there would be a provision available to pursue my vision. Faith was the lens for me to see it. Faith enabled me to choose my vision instead of a job that had accommodated obligations. Faith gave me the courage to submit my resignation. Faith provided me with courage to enroll as a full-time graduate student. And faith gave me the confidence and clarity to recognize an unexpected financial blessing.

God's unexpected blessing and provision was revealed as a financial award for my spouse. The award was given as a salary increase by his employer for a specific period of time. Incredibly, this specific period of time was parallel to the time needed to complete my strategic vision map. My faith was the means for God to respond with a provision. My story is not meant to suggest that every faith encounter will produce a similar outcome, but faith is a means for divine intervention, and can be the means for a desired result. The important takeaway is to make sure you have sufficient financial resources not allocated to existing obligations, that can support current and anticipated needs through the completion of your vision. Finally, recognize your faith as a powerful and viable resource.

The fourth and final function of the mapping cloud is to confirm your timing. Your timing is confirmed by completing the action steps within the mapping cloud. By completing these action steps, you advance your workable strategy to achieve your vision. Your timing is not based solely on having verified your vision and starting point or having secured the financial resources. Your timing is also based on your spiritual, physical, and mental readiness to navigate each of the steps of your strategic vision map. All factor into the process of confirming your timing, and God's timing, and determine the delivery of His plan and the achievement of your vision.

As you will recall, I shared with you that I am a planner of everything. However, just because I had a plan did not mean it was the right time to move forward. After verifying my vision of Chaplain ministry, I began a difficult clinical training process to advance and achieve my vision. As a Chaplain resident, I was required to complete 40-hours-of clinical training each week, and a 32-hour on-call rotation to staff emergencies. This rigorous schedule was intensified by a daily 4-hour commute to and from the Medical Center. Unfortunately, my clinical training did not exempt me from my other responsibilities of being a wife, mother, and associate minister in my faith community. Looking back, the intensity of my schedule should have caused me to pause. I was in over my head, with a myriad of personal and professional responsibilities, and was incapable of setting priorities. That was because of a deep sense of obligation to all of these roles. If I had taken a much-needed pause, then I could have possibly identified a workable strategy to manage my physical health, and spiritual well-being. More importantly, a brief pause would have confirmed it was not the right timing. But my eagerness to begin living the vision had caused me to start prematurely. Premature starts are a result of your failure to confirm your timing. They can create unwanted delays and hinder progress in advancing and achieving your vision. This is where I had misjudged my readiness and preparation. Although, I had verified the vision and starting point, and identified the financial resources, I had failed to confirm the timing. Planning is necessary to execute a strategic vision map, but confirming the timing is essential to its achievement. When you confirm your timing, you are indicating your complete capacity to achieve your vision.

―――――

The scripture at the onset of this chapter poses a question for contemplation. *What* was Jesus teaching His Disciples about faith? *Is* it the means for God's supernatural power? The simple answer is *yes*. Although the disciples were eyewitnesses to Jesus' faith, they lacked the understanding that the source of its power and authority came from God. True faith comes from God and is a gift. It is developed in the heart by the power of the Holy Spirit, and transforms the believer's life, and their perception of the intangible. Faith enables all believers to pursue God for all things, even those things that seem impossible. Therefore, the lesson Jesus was teaching His disciples, then and now, is to have irrefutable faith that glorifies God and satisfies His will, purpose, and plans for you.

6

KEEP MOVING

Keeping The Vision Within Reach

———

Then He said, "Go out, and stand on the mountain before the Lord." And behold, the Lord passed by, and a great and strong wind tore into the mountains and broke the rocks in pieces before the Lord, but the Lord was not in the wind; and after the wind an earthquake, but the Lord was not in the earthquake; and after the earthquake a fire, but the Lord was not in the fire; and after the fire a still small voice. (1 Kings 19:11-12)

In beginning this chapter, I want to jump right into the scripture and its meaningfulness to this discussion. Here is the back-story: (1 Kings 18-19) God handed the prophet Elijah a supernatural victory in a showdown with four hundred and fifty false prophets of the pagan god Baal. These false prophets were servants to King Ahab and his Queen Jezebel. She was the one who held the fear of the people. Jezebel had single-handedly orchestrated a massacre of the Lord's prophets. What is surprising about this story is its conclusion. After learning that Elijah had executed her prophets, Jezebel sent him a message threatening his demise. Elijah, instead of taking a victory lap in faith and fortitude, ran for his life and eventually sought refuge in a cave. Weakened by fear and fatigue, Elijah heard God. It was not in a spectacular theophany but in a still, small voice. Elijah heard both calm and command as God spoke to him that it was not the time to rest, but to press onward.

The significance of Elijah's story is that it demonstrates how no one is exempt from trials when they are pursuing a triumph. There is always the chance you will have your own personal experiences with Jezebels who will threaten you with defeat and provoke you to fear. You must not lose your focus. You must keep your vision within your reach. You do this by making an investment in your relationship with

God. It is God who affirms His plans for you, and divinely intervenes to ensure they are not derailed by threats of failure but are driven by provisions of promise. Elijah's victory serves as a reminder to keep moving forward with courageous faith and focus on God's plan to achieve your vision.

———

The strategic vision map (see Illustration 3, Appendix) has at the base of the vision halo a series of motion arrows. These motion arrows indicate the direction in which you should be progressing at various stages on your strategic vision map. In looking at the strategic vision map illustration, note the motion arrow marked *start point* is flanked by two smaller arrows. These smaller arrows represent the completion of qualifying tasks. As this relates to my strategic vision map, the smaller motion arrows are indicators that I had reviewed my past experiences to gain insight, clarified my call, narrowed the focus of my vision, and evaluated my strategic planning to gain perspective on specific action steps. By completing all of these qualifying tasks, I was able to advance to the next progressive step and draw the *start point* motion arrow.

The *start-point* motion arrow is a visual of *where* to start. It is positioned on the strategic vision map as a result of clarified information from the completion of qualifying tasks. Similarly, the smaller motion arrows in the illustration are a visual of the qualifying tasks. Once you have clarified information to qualify your start point motion arrow, then you can begin working on the action steps of the *goal-driven task* motion arrow. Your completion of each motion arrow is marked progress in achieving your vision.

The *goal-driven task* motion arrow identifies specific action steps. As it pertains to my strategic vision map, these action steps were succinct, adaptable, and qualified. This meant there was no guessing on actions needed to advance my strategic goals. The first action step required submitting an application to seminary. For example, my application was carefully constructed with information drawn from the completion of the qualifying tasks, my past experiences, and the clarity I had of my vision. Remember, at that time my vision was only defined as a ministry leader. The application was important because it would be the instrument of introduction. Therefore, my vision and desired result would need to be well-defined prior to the admission interview.

This is why it is important to work through the qualifying tasks, so you will know *what* you are trying to achieve.

The second action step was to increase the probability of being admitted to seminary. My approach was to utilize skills learned from previous interviews with potential employers. This meant I would need to lean in to personal and professional characteristics that represented the best version of myself. Clarifying these characteristics included reviewing previous successes and failures and completing mock interviews to sharpen my skills. My strategy was to apply intentional actions to achieve all identified goal driven tasks.

The third action step was to be strategic with *how* and *when* to use my resources, and support systems to graduate with my Divinity degree. As you will recall, I have noted how important finances are to achieve your vision. Securing financial resources will require ongoing strategic planning and consequent actions. Don't disregard the resources you have within your circle of family, friends and colleagues. These are people who can support your unanticipated absence or fill in for you when there is a schedule conflict. Circles of support are invaluable resources, especially when you need to fulfill existing obligations. As you can see, each action step is a process of qualifying the position of each motion arrow to keep you moving towards the achievement of your vision.

The process of *affirmation* will be discussed in greater detail in Chapter 7. For this discussion, affirmation will be in the context of its motion arrow. The affirmation motion arrow labeled to the right exterior of the vision halo, was qualified by the identification of resources that justify your progression forward. Note that the placement of the affirmation motion arrow on the strategic vision map is unique. Although its motion is upward, it is also continuous. This is because in the vision mapping process, resources are not strictly objective but are also subjective. For example, your faith in God for the provision of resources is considered subjective, and yet, faith should be a key factor of your planning. The takeaway from this simple snapshot of the motion arrows is they are essential to advancing strategic actions to achieve your vision.

———

In complete transparency, I remember being nervous

about taking that first action step. This is because taking action on your strategic vision map requires courageous faith. There were a lot of *what ifs* that flooded my thoughts, and I questioned everything. Fear can lead you to second-guess whether all of your preparation is enough to fulfill your vision, and for me, the questions were stifling. What if my undergraduate grades weren't good enough to be admitted? What if the interview didn't go well and I wasn't accepted as a degree candidate? What if the seminary wanted references to attest to my pastoral ministry capability? This questioning of myself created stress, doubt, and discouragement. However, by focusing on the exhaustive planning used to create a strategic vision map that would ultimately produce my desired result, I was able to resolve unacknowledged fear. Fear had become an obstacle for me to achieve my vision. But until I was able to name it as fear, I was hindered by my own thoughts of what was impossible instead of what was possible. My point is that courage and confidence come with knowing God as the source of all you desire. Even though the vision is yours, the plan is His. Remember, Elijah became fearful only when he believed he was alone, and the only prophet left alive. In Elijah's moment of fear, he forgot God was his greatest resource. The only question you should have as you begin your action steps is *why* am I here? In contrast to Elijah, your answer should attest to the hope you have within you. You must remain steadfast with courage and confidence that you will achieve your vision.

The insight gained from my experiences was when you pursue your vision, you must be intentional in creating a thorough plan that tells you *where, when,* and *how* to be successful. Therefore, pray for the vision, plan the vision, and plot the vision into a workable strategy that you can visualize on a strategic vision map. Remember, your detailed vision map includes task motion arrows that will guide you and affirm alignment with God's plan.

7

FINISHING WELL
The Faith To Finish

Now faith is the substance of things hoped for,

the evidence of things not seen. (Hebrews 11:1)

With graduation, degree conferment, ordination, Chaplain residency, and endorsement completed, I was leaning into fully realizing my vision in ministry as a professional Chaplain. All of these completed tasks were marked with God's affirmation. Faith gave me the hope to see my vision as a part of God's preeminent plan. It is a true measure of your faith when you see your hope unfold as an achieved vision. Faith had been a definitive part of my plans in pursuing my vision. God had transformed my plan of what I wanted for my life into ministry and mission. But faith only materializes as something real when you trust and believe that God can make it happen. I had actually made it to the finish line. And you will make it to the finish line too. It will require every degree of creativity you can muster, and every ounce of faith within you.

As an analogy, think of well-trained athletes in an Olympic Games 200 Meter event. These athletes are physically and mentally conditioned to compete in the race for a chance at their dream. However, like the spectators watching the race, these athletes know some competitors won't finish the race at all. Although these competing athletes have strategically planned to navigate the course successfully, some will be overcome by physical and mental fatigue, fall behind the leading pack, and in the last moments give up. This is why it is important that you prepare strategically, physically, spiritually, and emotionally to achieve your vision. Even though your detailed strategic vision plan appears ironclad, make sure it is vetted in faith, developed according to God's plan, and affirmed by both provision and opportunity. All of these *small fine print* details prepare you to cross the finish line.

Affirmation in the process of strategic vision mapping is important. It is important because it signals you have actual access to the resources and opportunities needed to fully execute your vision. How you achieve affirmation is a process and determining the specific stages of progression can be challenging. This is because affirmation, in the context of this discussion, is a principle of faith. It also means your progression may be unanticipated instead of calculated.

The first stage of affirmation is to gain access to provisions. This occurs when you use a combination of skill, strategy, and resources to identify or recognize an opportunity. Using my story, I had completed all the mapped tasks leading to this point. I was prepared and ready to begin working as a professional Chaplain. The provision I needed was access to a vacant Chaplain position in a healthcare institution or organization, and this had not happened yet in my process. Unfortunately, all of my networking efforts with Chaplains and Spiritual Care Managers were unsuccessful, and both groups were identified as resources to advance my progression to achieve my vision. I had to avoid dwelling on my lack of success in networking, and not allow the loss of these resources to become a deterrent. I had calculated cooperative networking as the next progressive step to a Chaplain position, but failed. I was struggling with feelings of defeat, but my faith was the principle that affirmed God could make it happen for me. Although unanticipated, God created a fully unmasked provision.

This provision came about when a ministry colleague in my Chaplain residency group shared that she had interviewed for a position, and thought it was better suited for me than it was for her. She made this determination based on her knowledge of my past experiences and considered my skills the best match. Although equally qualified, my colleague who was competing for Chaplain positions chose to advocate on my behalf. In doing so, she created an opportunity and the provision I needed to finish the final tasks of my strategic vision map. Keep in mind, a provision may not be visibly evident or may be delivered by proxy, but it is still meant solely for you. This is what it means for God to affirm what He makes possible as a result of faith, persistence, and resilience.

The second stage of affirmation is to recognize opportunities that provide the means to realizing your vision. Having the means to accomplish your vision does not mean you become short-sighted. Your actions will need to be deliberate when your vision is within reach. This is the time to apply all of your expertise and skills to create momentum. In my case, although my colleague had advocated for my candidacy with a potential employer, she was not the best spokesperson for me. She was unable to present a complete or accurate depiction because she did not have full knowledge of my expertise, education, and experience, and how they shaped my vision. This is why it is important to remember, you are the best spokesperson you can have for yourself. Self-advocating has nothing to do with having a lack of humility, but everything to do with having a confident faith. My opportunity presented itself through an advocate and God had designated it for me in faithful fulfillment of my vision. Nevertheless, I needed to take the lead in procuring it. And by doing so, I became gainfully employed as a Chaplain for the first time.

Providing you with the best opportunities is at the heart of God's affirmation, and this is what makes it possible for you to succeed in attaining your vision. Reflecting back to the pursuit of my vision, I recognize there were times when I endured physical and mental fatigue. Although I was not necessarily aware this was happening, every failed attempt to network or wrangle my way into a Chaplain position was a blow to my spiritual and emotional psyche. My faith was the factor that helped me stay the course to the finish line. As a final note to you on affirmation, it is your faith that will give you that final burst of adrenaline to lean into the final stretch. You must push through to the finish and forsake fatigue and fear, and finish well with your vision captured and God's plan complete.

8

FINALLY, BUT NOT FINISHED
Succession Planning

———

Delight yourself also in the Lord, And He shall give you the desires of your heart. (Psalms 37:4)

The scripture that frames this concluding chapter has a central theme of divine favor and a directive to pursue the will of God with faith, trust, and obedience. The psalmist David who is credited with writing this psalm, reconciled that active obedience is a forerunner to divine favor. Divine favor can produce the desires of your heart. The back-story is that David was displeased with the appearance of divine favor for wrongdoers. David did not want the people of God to become weary in their well-doing. He encouraged the people to remain steadfast and examine their desires to ensure they were God-serving, and not motivated by worldly ambitions for success or satisfaction. God's desire is that we delight in our pursuit to do His will, and by doing so, we then reap the benefits of active obedience and service to Him. Thus, the desires of our heart should always be to first please God. Then pursue our vision and desired result as a part of God's plan and divine favor.

About two-and-a-half years after I retired from active Chaplain ministry, I was given an opportunity to serve as the administrator of Christian Education in a local church setting. Although I was grateful for the opportunity, I had already succeeded in achieving my vision and was ambivalent about committing to a new ministry assignment. Like many people, retirement was a time to rest and be free of any obligations and commitments to an employer. Honestly, this is how I had imagined my retirement. I would have complete freedom in my schedule. There would be no more 12-hour workdays or 3:00 a.m. emergency visits with patients or families in crisis. There would be no more unscheduled bereavement visits that disrupted my plans with my family or friends. And there would be no more early morning calls to caregivers or colleagues to encourage them so they could care for others. My retirement days were going to be whatever I chose, and if that was nothing at all, it would be alright with me. But in these early years of retirement, I learned God never forgets your prayers or petitions, even if you do.

Years before the Chaplain vision was clear, I had asked God for a position in Christian Education but had forgotten these prayers. Even though I had reached the point of rest and retirement, I could not reject the opportunity because God was answering a long-forgotten prayer and a desire of my heart.

Fast forward, two years, three months, and twenty-six days, and I was in the midst of a *succession plan* long forgotten but now being realized. The main purpose of the succession plan (see Illustration 4, Appendix) is to provide you with a visual of a future opportunity beyond the core vision of your strategic vision map. The function of succession planning is to develop a contingency plan with a core strategy of securing an opportunity in the future.

This future opportunity is usually most compatible with skills acquired from your diverse experiences, expertise, and training. Succession planning takes into consideration your overall potential for this opportunity and helps you organize a workable strategy inclusive of your personal strengths and capabilities. The uniqueness of the succession plan is that it is not subject to a specific timeframe and is flexible and adaptable.

In order to simplify the process of succession planning, I have condensed it into a working formula of the following key tasks:

1. Identify and evaluate your targeted market. Pay specific attention to opportunities that are a natural progression of your core vision and are suited to your capabilities.

2. Qualify your opportunities. Determine whether you meet criteria for the opportunities (i.e., experience, expertise, education, training, etc.) and whether there can be a mutual beneficial relationship or partnership with members of your targeted market.

3. Create a presence in areas of opportunity. Volunteer as a way to gain insight into whether there is compatibility with your skills, then narrow or redirect the focus of your strategy.

4. Determine if there are networking opportunities available. Stimulate mutual interest in collaborations and partnerships as a means of furthering your transitional planning.

The working formula outlined for completing the succession planning tasks were useful in identifying, evaluating, qualifying, and creating opportunities that were a natural progression of my core vision, and were well-suited to my capabilities. All of the know-how skills from my diverse experiences, the how-to skills from my organizational planning, and the can-do skills from my administrative experiences were a natural progression to a position in Christian Education. However, as I began working as the administrator, it became apparent that the position was far more complex than I had anticipated. This is why it is important to work through the succession planning tasks. It will help you accurately identify and qualify the opportunity as being aligned with your expectations as well as your capabilities. It will also ensure your success and help you navigate this stage of your life. Remember, this future opportunity is a part of God's plan for your vision. Although incorporating succession planning is optional to your strategic vision map, its inclusion is a step forward in your preparation for the future opportunities God has planned for your vision.

Once I had completed the final goal of my strategic vision map, I experienced a true sense of achievement. This achievement was marked by new opportunities in my succession plan. What I learned as a result of my pursuit of God's plan and my vision, is that with each progressive step taken to advance my strategic vision map, I was equipped with more spiritual insight. As a result of my progress, God had created new variations of my spiritual blueprint, and each represented a new opportunity for future goals.

As you prepare to develop your strategic vision map, remember your map will evolve as a result of the process of clarifying your goals, a starting point, resources, and a sequence of steps. Keep in mind that spiritual insight is an invaluable resource used to develop a workable strategy to align your vision with God's plan. Your progression through these stages will help you visualize the *small fine print* and the strategies for achieving your vision as the desired result. Therefore, be deliberate in creating your strategic vision map as a well-planned strategy that is executed in faith and you will realize your vision.

GLOSSARY OF TERMS

Affirmation – As it pertains to vision mapping, it is having real access to existing resources and opportunities needed to fully execute the vision.

Aligned Plan – A vision plan being confirmed by divinely appointed provisions that are tangible, accessible, and available for the completion of tasks, goals, or assignments related to the achievement of your vision.

Developing Vision – An examination of key issues, personal aspirations, and spiritual insight to determine the concise focus of your vision and the desired result.

Divine Moment – An unanticipated period of time that is unique to God for the purpose of revealing to you the crucial parts of His plan for your vision. It is also a reference to the divinity of God. This phrase represents how God has historically communicated at times with His people, concerning His plans and their visions, dreams, and prayers.

Guiding Strategies – The compilation of key information from training, expertise, experiences, and influences to establish the parameters and approach for achieving specific goals or objectives for a desired result.

Mapping – The process that enables you to visualize your strategy and progressively align your vision. The process of mapping has four primary tasks: To help you clarify the specific goals of your vision; To help you to identify your starting point; To help you verify the resources needed to achieve the desired result; and To help you develop the sequence of steps and strategies necessary to see your vision goals through to successful completion.

Mapping Cloud – A visual tool used to cumulatively store the vision data and guiding strategies you will execute. It functions as a detailed checklist that identifies the sequence of steps, the resources available, and the optimal timing for engaging strategies to achieve your vision.

Ministry Gifts – Abilities or gifts of help that all Christian believers possess and share through acts of service and faithful obedience to God. These abilities or gifts are used both within and outside of the faith community, as a means of witnessing the faith of the Gospel and transforming lives for Christ Jesus.

Plan of Navigation – A strategy to achieve your vision with calculated, precise, and planned movements.

Providential Nature of God – The divine relationship between God and humanity and the blessings that relationship invites, as well as the help or divine intervention received from God.

Purposeful Plan – God's intended purpose for all human beings. It is revealed in part through divinely appointed moments and through faith to believers.

Qualifying Tasks – Specific tasks that provide insight, clarify information, and narrow the focus of actions needed to advance to the next progressive stage or step of the strategic vision map. Conclusion of these tasks is represented by the direction of a motion arrow.

Spiritual Blueprint – Your vision constructed by God and designed specifically for you. It materializes as a viable plan as a result of your immutable faith.

Strategic Guide – The guiding purpose of the strategic vision map.

Strategic Vision Map – The primary visual guide used to direct the vision process and troubleshoot potential issues that can delay your progression or hinder your ability to achieve your vision.

Succession plan – A contingency plan with a core strategy to secure an opportunity in the future that is most compatible with skills acquired from your diverse experiences, expertise, and training.

Visioning - The process of transforming your ideas (goals and objectives), dreams, or images of your future into tangible and functioning present actions or desired outcomes.

Vision Data – The data compiled based on training, expertise, past experiences, and influences, which you will use to develop a working strategy to successfully complete your strategic vision map.

Vision Halo – The task center of your vision map. It contains the specific tasks needed to achieve your vision. It has, at its center, your vision, the core goals needed to accomplish your vision, and goal-driven tasks that advance progressive action toward achieving your vision.

Vision Map - The blueprint of your vision. It is created by clarifying your goals, identifying your starting point, pinpointing your resources, planning the sequence of steps, and utilizing spiritual insight to align (confirm) your vision with God's plan.

Vision Plan - The strategy used to outline the core goals that guide you in making decisions to align your strategic vision map with God's plan.

Vision Strategy – The processes used to plan and create your vision map.

Visual Strategic Map – A visual aid that is used to guide you through a specific task.

Vision Template – The outline for your vision halo produced from experiential learning, self-reflection, and spiritual exploration, which all support your vision strategy and the specific task of clarifying information.

Workable Resources – Knowledge, skills, abilities, education, training, influences, experiences, people you know, and connections you have made. All of these are useful to you in the process of successfully completing the tasks or the goals of your strategic vision map.

Workable Strategy – A combination of corresponding actions to accomplish all goals needed to achieve your vision.

APPENDIX

VISION MAP
Illustrations 1-4

———

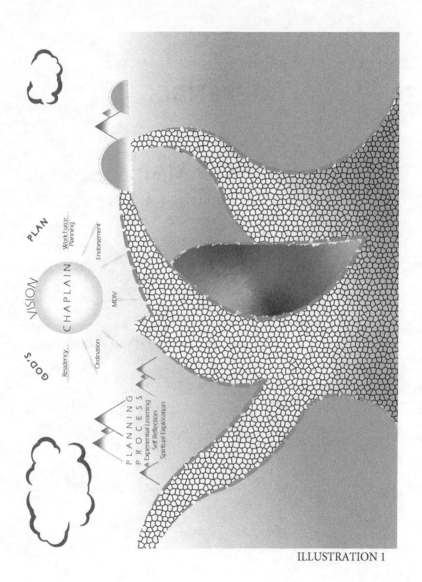

ILLUSTRATION 1

82

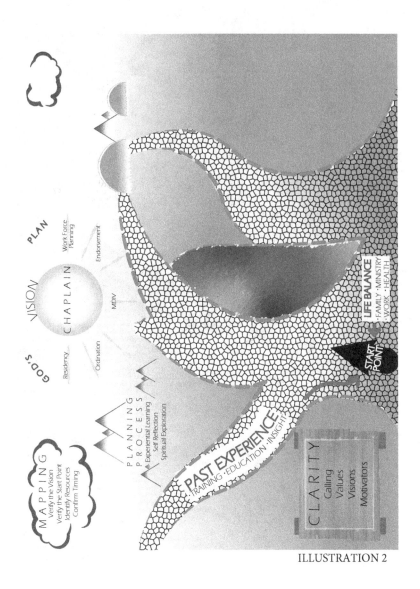

ILLUSTRATION 2

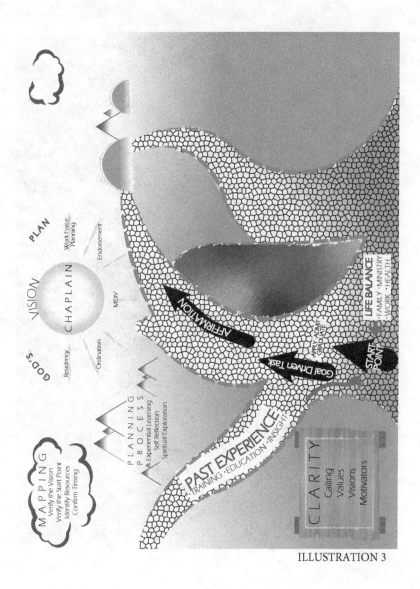

ILLUSTRATION 3

84

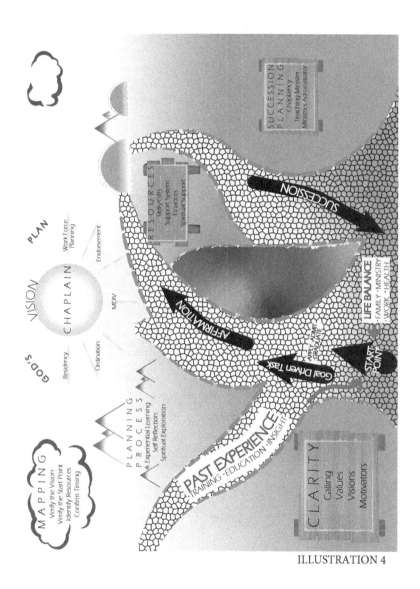

ILLUSTRATION 4

85

AFTERWORD

I began writing this book about three years ago at a time when the world was not in the midst of a pandemic. The Novel Coronavirus 2019, which is also known as COVID-19, has caused great pain, suffering, and hopelessness. However, it is not the only crisis the United States of America is facing. The United States is being struck and even paralyzed by the civil unrest of its citizens who have taken to the streets for months in protest. These protests were sparked by the death of an unarmed black man by a white police officer. A movement calling for local, state, federal, and political leaders to act justly and swiftly toward long-standing policies and practices that support systemic racism rather than racial reconciliation is sweeping across this nation. This is the timing of the launch of this book. Although I sought to keep focus on the content of the preceding pages,

I would be remiss to ignore the fact that at the heart of this book is a message of faith. Faith stands as a stark reminder that whether for a cure, a cause, or in the form of a vision, a sovereign God can restore the broken, heal the sick, reconcile our relationships, and redeem all that is lost.

Just think of what kind of nation and people we could be if we were all committed to justice and peace. Just think of the burdens that could be alleviated by eradicating the division and divisiveness of supremacy that has longed plagued our society. Just think of what we could accomplish by supporting the vision of people, black, brown, and beige, who cling to the hope of having unobstructed access to the inalienable rights guaranteed to all of the citizens of this great nation. This would truly be an exercise in aligning with God's plan.

Looking back over these past three years, it amazes me how many times I had spoken that one day I was going to write a book. Although this book was not initially meant to be instructive, my vision to become a Chaplain was more than a story. As I began to write, I realized that my story was about visualizing the *small fine print* as a faith driven strategic vision plan. It was hard work and tedious, but I needed to share the details of how to make a vision a reality. Yes, God made it all happen because I refused to be defeated by the challenges of being a woman in ministry with an overflowing plate of responsibilities. Most importantly, my story can be anyone's story as long as they are willing to invest themselves in the promises and plans of God.

There are so many things that are frightening when we do them for the very first time, and this book was definitely in that category for me. Sometimes, fear is what motivates you to get out of your own way, so you can help someone else find theirs. To this end, it is my hope that you have the courage to pursue God's plan to achieve your vision.

ACKNOWLEDGEMENTS

To my husband, Ron – You are the love of my life. Thank you for all of your unwavering support, the gourmet meals, and for the encouragement, space, and time to write.

To my children, Christopher, Bryan, and Demetria – Your examples of courage have always inspired me. Thank you for always encouraging me to write and tell my story. It is because of you that I am the best version of myself.

To my pastoral counselors and friends, Rev. Dr. Robert C. Jones, Jr. and Rev. Roxanne Cardenas – I know this very special thank you is not enough for all the hours, days, months, and years given to coaching me through writer's block and encouraging me to get out of my own way. I love you guys dearly.

To my training pastor, Rev. Dr. Leroy A. Mitchell – Thank you for believing in me and seeing what I could not at the time. The preparation was invaluable, and I will be forever grateful.

To my friend and editor, Jinx Smith Kenan – You are the best! Thank you for all the things you do that are too numerous to list.

To my artist, Mia Little, of Little Creative Designs, Illinois – You are absolutely amazing! Thank you for bringing my illustrations and book cover to life. They are more than I could have imagined.

To my friend and photographer, Sonia S. Williams – Thank you for the Tuesday Morning Praise Break and for always capturing the best of me.

To my friend and IT Technical Consultant, Anthony Sturdivant – Thank you for always taking my calls and walking me through the technical language and software applications so that it makes sense to me, because you know I am not tech savvy.

To my spiritual families, from the Midwest to the Southeast – I appreciate the love and support through the years.

And To My God – May all glory and honor be given to you for your goodness and faithfulness!